Morgan Wallen's Revolution

A Fresh Look

Jerry Clarke

Jerry Clarke

All rights reserved. No part of this publication may be reproduced, distributed, or transmitted in any form or by any means, including photocopying, recording, or other electronic or mechanical methods, without the prior written permission of the publisher, except in the case of brief quotations embodied in critical reviews and certain other noncommercial uses permitted by copyright law.

Copyright © Jerry Clarke 2023.

Morgan Wallen's Revolution: A Fresh Look

TABLE OF CONTENTS

CHAPTER 1: EARLY LIFE AND MUSICAL ROOTS

CHAPTER 2: NASHVILLE DREAMS

CHAPTER 3: CHART-TOPPING SUCCESS

CHAPTER 4: FACING ADVERSITY AND PERSONAL GROWTH

CHAPTER 5: A NEW LOOK, A NEW CHAPTER

CONCLUSION

Jerry Clarke

Chapter 1: Early Life and Musical Roots

Morgan Wallen's early life in the picturesque town of Sneedville, nestled in the Appalachian region of East Tennessee, provided the foundation for his remarkable journey in the world of music. Born on May 13, 1993, Wallen grew up surrounded by the breathtaking beauty of the mountains, but it was the harmonious melodies of his musical family that truly shaped his destiny.

In Sneedville, the Wallen family was known for their deep-rooted love for music. Morgan's father, a preacher at a local church, had a profound influence on him. The hymns and gospel tunes that echoed through the church's halls became the first notes that young Morgan would sing along to. These early experiences ignited a passion for music that would stay with him throughout his life.
Morgan's father, known to many as a preacher in their close-knit community in Sneedville, played a pivotal role in shaping not only Morgan's early life but also his passion for music and his unwavering determination to pursue his dreams. A pillar of faith and a source of inspiration, Morgan's father infused their household with a deep appreciation for gospel music and a strong moral compass.

As a preacher, he delivered powerful sermons that resonated with the congregation, emphasizing the importance of compassion, love, and the spiritual connection that music could bring. Morgan's father recognized the impact that music had on people's hearts and souls, and this realization fueled his support for Morgan's budding musical talents.

Gospel hymns and spiritual melodies filled the walls of their home, providing a harmonious backdrop to Morgan's formative years. These songs not only nurtured his musical abilities but also instilled in him a sense of purpose and a belief in the positive influence that music could have on others.

Morgan's father not only encouraged his son's musical interests but also provided guidance and moral grounding. He taught Morgan the value of hard work, honesty, and humility, qualities that would later become essential in navigating the challenges of the music industry. His father's unwavering support gave Morgan the confidence to pursue his dreams, even when the path seemed daunting.

Beyond the spiritual and moral guidance, Morgan's father was a source of strength during the early years of his musical journey. He attended Morgan's performances, offering encouragement and a sense of pride that bolstered Morgan's confidence. His presence in the audience, often accompanied by the rest of the family, reminded Morgan of the importance of staying true to his roots and the responsibility he felt to honor his hometown and family through his music.

From a young age, Wallen's talent as a singer was undeniable. His voice, a powerful and soulful instrument, seemed to defy his age. He was quickly recognized as a standout in the local community, drawing attention every time he sang in church or school events. His parents, recognizing his potential, nurtured his gift and encouraged him to pursue his musical aspirations.

Growing up in a household where music was not only appreciated but celebrated, Wallen was exposed to a diverse range of genres. While gospel music held a special place in his heart, he also listened to country classics, rock 'n' roll hits, and even some blues. This eclectic musical upbringing would later contribute to the unique blend of styles that would define his own music.

Wallen's exposure to gospel music left an indelible mark on him. The emotional depth and spiritual resonance of gospel tunes became a part of his musical DNA. The richness of these melodies, combined with the heartfelt lyrics, would later influence his songwriting, giving his country music a distinct emotional depth.

As Wallen entered his teenage years, he began to actively engage with music beyond the confines of his family and church. He joined the local church choir, where his exceptional vocal abilities shone brightly. His voice, filled with raw emotion and a maturity beyond his years, often left the congregation in awe. This experience not only allowed him to refine his singing skills but also introduced him to the power of connecting with an audience through music.

In addition to his involvement in the choir, Wallen picked up the guitar, a decision that would prove pivotal in his musical journey. He spent hours strumming the strings, teaching himself to play and experimenting with different chords and melodies. This newfound skill opened up a world of possibilities, enabling him to accompany his singing with the rhythmic beauty of the guitar.

By the time he reached high school, Wallen was already well-known in his community for his musical talents. He began performing at local events, and it became clear that he was destined for a future in music. However, Sneedville, while nurturing his early passion, was a small town with limited opportunities in the music industry. It was clear to Wallen that if he wanted to pursue his dreams on a larger stage, he would need to venture beyond the hills of East Tennessee.

With a heart full of determination and a guitar in hand, Wallen set his sights on Nashville, the epicenter of the country music universe. Nashville was a city with a rich history of nurturing aspiring musicians, a place where dreams had been realized for countless artists before him. The decision to leave his hometown was not easy, but Wallen knew it was a necessary step on his path to musical success.

As he arrived in Nashville, the challenges of pursuing a music career in a competitive city became apparent. The city's bustling music scene was filled with talented individuals, each vying for their moment in the spotlight. Wallen faced the same struggles that many aspiring musicians encounter: finding gigs, making connections, and honing his craft amidst the intensity of the industry.

He started by playing in small bars and clubs, gradually making a name for himself on the local circuit. It was during these intimate performances that Wallen's distinctive voice and energetic stage presence began to captivate audiences. His unique blend of country, rock, and gospel influences set him apart from the crowd, hinting at the potential for greatness that lay ahead.

While Nashville provided countless opportunities, it also presented its share of setbacks. Rejections and disappointments were part of the journey, but Wallen remained resilient. He used these challenges as motivation to improve and refine his skills, and he dedicated himself to becoming not just a good singer, but a great artist.

During this time, Wallen also focused on his songwriting. Drawing inspiration from his own experiences and the stories of the people he met along the way, he began to craft heartfelt and relatable lyrics. His songs were a reflection of his roots, resonating with the authenticity of small-town life, love, and the struggles that come with chasing a dream.

While the road to success in Nashville was filled with ups and downs, Wallen's determination and passion for music sustained him. He embraced every opportunity to perform, continuously improving his stage presence and connecting with fans on a deeper level. The lessons he learned during this formative period would serve as the building blocks for his future achievements.

As Wallen navigated the challenges of Nashville, he remained grounded in his East Tennessee upbringing. The values instilled in him by his family and community were the bedrock of his character, and he carried those values with him as he pursued his musical aspirations. The small-town roots that shaped his early life would become an integral part of his identity as an artist, setting him on a course to leave a lasting impact on the world of country music.

In the midst of the competitive Nashville scene, Wallen's unique voice, combined with his passion for storytelling through music, was starting to gain recognition. While he hadn't yet reached the pinnacle of success, the foundations were firmly in place. Chapter 1 of Morgan Wallen's biography is a testament to the power of early influences, the importance of family, and the resilience required to chase one's dreams. It's a chapter filled with the hope and promise of a young musician on the verge of something great, ready to make his mark on the world of country music.

Jerry Clarke

Chapter 2: Nashville Dreams

The moment Morgan Wallen set foot in Nashville, he embarked on a transformative journey through the heart of the country music industry. This chapter delves into the early days of his Nashville experience, highlighting the challenges he faced, the opportunities he seized, and the unwavering determination that propelled him forward.

Nashville, often referred to as "Music City," is a place where aspiring musicians from all corners of the country converge, seeking to make their mark on the iconic musical landscape. For Wallen, this vibrant city was both exhilarating and daunting, offering a chance to chase his dreams but also presenting the reality of a competitive environment that demanded talent, perseverance, and the willingness to push beyond one's comfort zone.

In the early stages of his Nashville journey, Wallen faced the task of establishing himself within the local music scene. The city was filled with talented musicians, all striving for recognition in a city that was legendary for its songwriters, performers, and music industry professionals. It was a place where countless dreams were born, but only a select few would see those dreams come to fruition.

Wallen's first challenge was finding gigs. He quickly learned that getting stage time in Nashville was no easy feat. The competition was fierce, and established venues often favored acts with proven track records or strong connections. Undeterred, Wallen persevered, tirelessly reaching out to venues, attending open mic nights, and putting himself out there in the hopes of securing opportunities to showcase his unique talent.

The small bars and clubs of Nashville became his testing grounds, the places where he honed his craft and gained valuable experience as a performer. Night after night, he would take the stage, pouring his heart and soul into each performance. It was here that Wallen's distinctive voice, characterized by its soulful depth and emotive power, began to captivate audiences, setting him apart from the crowd.

Despite the challenges of the Nashville music scene, Wallen's passion for music burned brighter than ever. His resilience in the face of rejection and his relentless pursuit of his dreams mirrored the values instilled by his family and the small-town roots that shaped him. Each setback was a lesson, and each performance was a chance to refine his skills, connect with audiences, and prove that he belonged on this grand stage.

While navigating the intricate network of Nashville's music industry, Wallen also recognized the importance of building relationships and making meaningful connections. He understood that success often hinged on more than just raw talent; it required the ability to network, collaborate, and create a strong support system within the industry.

Wallen's dedication to his craft and his engaging personality gradually started to pay off. He began to make connections with fellow musicians, songwriters, and industry professionals. These relationships opened doors, providing him with opportunities to co-write songs, collaborate on projects, and gain insights into the inner workings of the music business. Through these interactions, Wallen continued to refine his songwriting skills and expand his musical horizons.

One of the pivotal moments during this chapter of Wallen's journey was his decision to audition for a popular reality TV show, "The Voice." While not everyone in the music industry views reality TV competitions as the ideal path to success, Wallen recognized it as an opportunity to reach a wider audience and gain valuable exposure. His appearance on "The Voice" brought his talent to the attention of a broader demographic, enabling him to showcase his powerful vocals and stage presence on a national platform.

Although he didn't win the competition, his time on "The Voice" proved to be a stepping stone in his career. It exposed him to a larger audience and solidified his determination to pursue a music career at the highest level. The experience also provided him with valuable insights into the dynamics of the entertainment industry, preparing him for the challenges and opportunities that lay ahead.

Following his time on "The Voice," Wallen's talent and potential didn't go unnoticed. He caught the attention of industry insiders and eventually signed with Big Loud Records, a prominent Nashville label. This partnership marked a significant milestone in his journey, giving him the resources and support he needed to further his career.

As Wallen's profile continued to rise, he released a series of successful singles that resonated with country music fans and showcased his dynamic musical style. "Whiskey Glasses," a standout hit, showcased his ability to tell heartfelt stories through his music, and "Up Down," a collaboration with Florida Georgia Line, solidified his position as a rising star in the genre.

These early successes validated Wallen's decision to pursue his dreams in Nashville. He was no longer just a young artist trying to find his place; he was a recognized talent making waves in the country music scene. The challenges he faced in the city had strengthened his resolve, and his authenticity as a storyteller with a unique voice had captured the hearts of fans and industry professionals alike.

In addition to his music, Wallen's image and persona began to take shape during this period. His distinct look, marked by his signature mullet hairstyle, became a recognizable part of his brand. However, it was his genuine personality, his relatability, and his openness about his roots and experiences that endeared him to his growing fan base. Wallen was a representation of the down-to-earth, small-town values that resonated with many, a true embodiment of the country spirit.

As this chapter of Wallen's biography concludes, the stage is set for even greater accomplishments. He has established himself as a rising star in Nashville, earning recognition for his vocal prowess, his captivating performances, and his ability to connect with audiences on a personal level. The challenges of the early days in Nashville have shaped him, preparing him for the next phase of his journey, where he will face new opportunities, new obstacles, and new milestones in his quest to become a country music legend.

Morgan Wallen's Revolution: A Fresh Look

Chapter 3: Chart-Topping Success

As Morgan Wallen's journey through the competitive landscape of Nashville continued, the next chapter of his biography marked a turning point. This phase of his career was characterized by chart-topping success, the release of impactful albums, the expansion of his fan base, and the evolution of his artistic identity.

Wallen's signing with Big Loud Records in Nashville was a pivotal moment that laid the foundation for his upward trajectory. The support and resources provided by the label allowed him to focus on his craft, collaborate with talented songwriters and producers, and create music that resonated with a wide audience.

One of the defining moments during this period was the release of Wallen's debut album, "If I Know Me." The album dropped on April 27, 2018, marking a significant milestone in his career. This collection of songs showcased Wallen's range as an artist, featuring a blend of catchy, radio-friendly tracks and heartfelt ballads that delved into themes of love, heartache, and the rollercoaster of life.

The album's lead single, "Up Down," a collaboration with Florida Georgia Line, had already achieved commercial success before the album's release, but it was the other tracks on "If I Know Me" that truly showcased Wallen's artistry. Songs like "Whiskey Glasses" and "Chasin' You"

Jerry Clarke

captured the attention of country music fans, with their relatable lyrics and Wallen's distinct vocal delivery.

"Whiskey Glasses" in particular struck a chord with listeners, becoming a massive hit on country radio. The song's clever and introspective lyrics, combined with Wallen's emotive performance, earned him a place in the hearts of fans across the nation. It was a breakthrough moment that solidified his status as a rising star in the country music scene.

The success of "If I Know Me" extended beyond individual tracks. The album as a whole received positive reviews from both critics and fans, earning Wallen a reputation as a talented artist capable of delivering a compelling and cohesive body of work. The album's themes of self-discovery, love, and youthful exuberance resonated with a broad audience, propelling Wallen into the spotlight.

In addition to his album's success, Wallen's live performances continued to capture the attention of music lovers. His energetic stage presence, charismatic personality, and powerful vocals made him a sought-after act in the country music circuit. Whether he was performing at small venues or sharing the stage with industry veterans, Wallen's ability to connect with audiences was undeniable.

The dedication and passion that Wallen brought to his performances were a testament to his roots and his desire to honor the traditions of country music. He understood the importance of authenticity and staying true to the values that shaped him. The connection he shared with fans during his live shows created a sense of camaraderie, making them feel like they were part of a shared experience.

As his popularity grew, Wallen also became a fixture on country music award shows and television specials. His appearances on major platforms allowed him to showcase his talents to an even broader audience, gaining recognition from both industry insiders and casual music fans. His charisma and down-to-earth personality made him a beloved figure in the country music community, and he was often lauded for his genuine and relatable nature.

However, as Wallen's star continued to rise, he faced a new set of challenges, including the scrutiny that comes with fame. Maintaining a sense of authenticity while navigating the pressures of the music industry and the public eye was no easy feat. Wallen's personal life and choices occasionally made headlines, but he remained steadfast in his commitment to his music and his dedication to his fans.

The support of his family, the lessons learned from his small-town upbringing, and the grounding influence of his father remained crucial in these moments. Wallen's authenticity and willingness to take responsibility for his actions endeared him to those who believed in his talent and recognized his genuine desire to make meaningful contributions to the world of country music.

As the chapter progresses, Wallen's artistic growth and creative evolution become evident. He continued to refine his songwriting skills, drawing from personal experiences and a deep well of emotions. His music became a platform for storytelling, a way to connect with listeners on a profound level by sharing the highs and lows of his own journey.

Wallen's sophomore album, "Dangerous: The Double Album," released in January 2021, marked a significant milestone in his career. This ambitious project showcased Wallen's growth as an artist and his willingness to push boundaries. The double album format allowed him to explore a diverse range of styles, themes, and emotions, revealing the many facets of his musical personality.

The album was met with critical acclaim and soared to the top of the charts, cementing Wallen's position as one of the hottest acts in country music. Its massive success was a testament to the connection he had forged with fans and the appeal of his honest and relatable songwriting. The album's lead single, "7 Summers," became another hit, further solidifying Wallen's presence on country radio.

"Dangerous: The Double Album" was a reflection of Wallen's artistic vision and his desire to create music that resonated with his audience. He took risks, experimented with different sounds, and showcased his growth as a songwriter and performer. The album's impact went beyond just the charts; it was a statement of Wallen's commitment to pushing the boundaries of what country music could be while staying true to its core values.

In the midst of his soaring career, Wallen remained grounded in his roots and connected with his fan base on a personal level. His interactions with fans, both online and at live events, highlighted his appreciation for their support and his genuine desire to share his music with those who believed in him. He recognized the importance of giving back and making a positive impact on the lives of those who looked up to him.

This chapter of Wallen's biography exemplifies the power of perseverance, the impact of chart-topping success, and the challenges that come with fame. It's a story of an artist who emerged from a small town in Tennessee, faced the trials of a competitive industry, and used his authentic voice to connect with a wide and passionate audience. As Wallen's career continued to ascend, he was poised to leave an indelible mark on the world of country music, setting the stage for even greater achievements in the chapters that lay ahead.

Chapter 4: Facing Adversity and Personal Growth

The road to success in the music industry is paved with peaks and valleys, and for Morgan Wallen, Chapter 4 of his biography encapsulates a period of both triumphs and challenges. As his career continued to ascend, he found himself facing adversity, making headlines for more than just his music, and embarking on a journey of personal growth and self-discovery.

With chart-topping albums and hit singles under his belt, Wallen had solidified his position as one of the hottest names in country music. He was a fan favorite, with a dedicated following that resonated with his heartfelt lyrics and charismatic performances. However, as he navigated the spotlight, he encountered a series of controversies that tested his resolve and required him to confront his actions and their impact on his career and personal life.

In early 2021, a significant controversy erupted around Morgan Wallen, thrusting him into the center of a media firestorm. The catalyst for this controversy was the emergence of a video in which Wallen was heard using a racial slur. This video, which quickly circulated on social media platforms, captured a private moment in which Wallen used offensive language, sparking widespread outrage and discussions about racial insensitivity.

The use of a racial slur is considered deeply offensive and inappropriate, as it perpetuates harmful stereotypes, fosters division, and contributes to a culture of intolerance. The swift and intense public reaction to the video was a direct result of the sensitivity surrounding such language and the awareness of its potential impact, particularly in the context of Wallen's public figure status.

As a prominent figure in the country music industry, Wallen's actions were subject to scrutiny not only from the general public but also from the media, fellow artists, and industry professionals. His use of the racial slur in the video not only shocked many but also led to significant consequences within the music community.

Several radio stations immediately removed Wallen's music from their playlists, and he faced disqualification from award shows, including the Academy of Country Music Awards. The consequences were not limited to the country music world; they extended to the broader entertainment industry, as Wallen's actions raised questions about the responsibility of artists and the impact of their behavior on their careers and public perception.

Wallen's swift and unequivocal response to the controversy was essential. He issued a public apology, acknowledging the hurt caused by his words and taking full responsibility for his actions. He expressed deep regret and a commitment to learning from his mistake, demonstrating a willingness to educate himself about the implications of the racial slur and to take steps towards personal growth and understanding.

The controversy surrounding Wallen's use of the racial slur brought to the forefront broader discussions about racial sensitivity, the role of celebrities in promoting inclusivity, and the importance of holding individuals accountable for their actions. It also highlighted the power of social media to disseminate information and spark conversations on critical societal issues.

Wallen's actions during this period, including his genuine apology and efforts to educate himself, were pivotal in shaping the narrative surrounding the controversy. While he faced criticism and consequences, his response also provided an opportunity for personal growth, self-reflection, and the commitment to being a more responsible and empathetic public figure.

The incident serves as a cautionary tale about the impact of one's actions, especially for individuals in the public eye. It underscores the need for continuous education and awareness, as well as the importance of using one's platform to promote positive change and inclusivity. Wallen's experience, as challenging as it was, provides valuable lessons for individuals in similar positions, emphasizing the significance of accountability, empathy, and a commitment to fostering understanding and unity.

The controversy thrust Wallen into a pivotal moment in his career, forcing him to confront the consequences of his words and actions. It was a challenging time, as he faced criticism, disappointment, and the realization that he had hurt people with his insensitive language. However, it was also an opportunity for growth, self-reflection, and learning from mistakes.

In the face of adversity, Wallen took responsibility for his actions, offering a public apology and taking steps to educate himself about the impact of racial slurs and the importance of promoting inclusivity and understanding. He

Morgan Wallen's Revolution: A Fresh Look

recognized that he had a platform and a responsibility to use it in a positive way, and he vowed to do better.

This chapter of Wallen's biography highlights the power of accountability and the resilience needed to overcome setbacks. It wasn't just about making amends; it was about demonstrating genuine change through actions and a commitment to fostering a more inclusive environment in the music industry and beyond. Wallen's journey of self-improvement and personal growth during this period became an essential part of his story, demonstrating that growth is a continuous process, and mistakes can serve as valuable lessons.

Amidst the challenges he faced, Wallen also continued to release music that resonated with fans. His sophomore album, "Dangerous: The Double Album," remained a hit, with songs like "Sand in My Boots" and "Wasted on You" capturing the hearts of listeners. The album's success demonstrated that, despite the controversies, his music remained a powerful force, connecting with people on an emotional level.

As Wallen navigated this complex chapter of his career, he leaned on the support of his family, friends, and those who believed in his ability to overcome adversity. His small-town roots, the lessons from his father, and the values instilled in him during his upbringing provided a foundation of strength. He recognized the importance of surrounding himself with positive influences and relying on the love and understanding of those who knew him best.

In addition to his personal growth, Wallen's music continued to evolve, showcasing his versatility as an artist. He explored new themes, experimented with different sounds, and maintained a commitment to authenticity in his songwriting. His ability to capture the essence of real-life experiences, from heartbreak to celebration, made him a relatable figure for fans across the country.

Wallen's authenticity was also evident in his collaborations. He teamed up with fellow artists, both established and emerging, to create memorable duets and joint performances. These partnerships allowed him to connect with a broader audience, introduce his music to new listeners, and demonstrate his commitment to the country music community.

While the challenges of this chapter were significant, Wallen's resilience and commitment to growth were evident. He used the adversity he faced as a catalyst for change, turning a moment of reckoning into an opportunity to become a better person and a more responsible artist. This period of self-discovery, humility, and the recognition of the importance of using his platform for positive change would go on to shape his trajectory in the industry.

As Chapter 4 concludes, Wallen's story is far from over. He has weathered storms, confronted personal challenges, and emerged with a renewed sense of purpose. His music, his willingness to learn from his mistakes, and his dedication to promoting a more inclusive and understanding environment serve as a testament to his growth as an artist and as an individual. The next chapters of his biography will reveal how he continues to navigate the ever-evolving music industry, leaving a lasting impact on the country music landscape while staying true to the lessons learned from his experiences.

Chapter 5: A New Look, A New Chapter

Morgan Wallen, the country sensation known not only for his music but also for his distinctive mullet hairstyle, surprised fans and created waves of conversation when he unveiled a dramatic change in his appearance during a recent concert in Columbus, Ohio. This moment marked not just a new look for Wallen but also a symbolic transition in his evolving journey as an artist.

The iconic mullet had become synonymous with Wallen's image over the years, a bold style choice that made him easily recognizable and set him apart in the country music scene. In an interview, Wallen shared that the inspiration for the mullet came from his father, who had sported the same hairstyle when he was Wallen's age. It was a nod to his roots and a way to connect with his family's history, reflecting the close-knit values that had shaped him.

Initially, Wallen's unconventional hairstyle wasn't met with unanimous approval. His management team and record label, Big Loud Label, had reservations about the mullet, unsure if it would align with the image they wanted to project. However, as time passed, the mullet grew on Wallen's colleagues, and it began to solidify as a defining part of his brand. Fans enthusiastically embraced the look, showing up to his concerts donning mullets and cutoff flannels, a testament to the impact he had on his audience.

But life, as we all know, is full of changes. Wallen's recent decision to shave off his signature mullet was met with mixed reactions from his devoted fanbase. While some expressed their disappointment, lamenting the loss of the beloved mullet, others supported Wallen's choice, recognizing that a shaved head would provide comfort during the sweltering summer months.

The decision to bid farewell to the mullet marked a significant moment in Wallen's career. It was not just a change in appearance; it was a symbol of evolution, a willingness to embrace change, and a reminder that an artist's journey is marked by continuous growth. Wallen's journey was no stranger to change; he had faced challenges, learned from his mistakes, and actively sought redemption after the controversy earlier in the year.

Morgan Wallen's Revolution:A Fresh Look

In the midst of the media firestorm and personal growth, Wallen's music remained a constant force. His songs continued to resonate with fans, offering comfort, inspiration, and a sense of connection. His live performances remained powerful, showcasing his growth as a performer, and providing fans with unforgettable experiences that transcended any particular hairstyle.

Throughout this chapter, Wallen's journey exemplified resilience and the ability to adapt. He had faced setbacks and controversy, but he confronted them head-on, demonstrating a commitment to becoming a better person and artist. His actions spoke volumes about his character, his desire to learn from his mistakes, and his aspiration to use his platform for positive change.

As the curtain closed on this chapter, Wallen's willingness to embrace a new look was a testament to his journey, showcasing his ability to evolve while staying true to his roots. The conversation surrounding his haircut became a talking point among his fans, highlighting his impact and his continued growth as an artist.

Wallen's journey wasn't just about his music and image; it was also about his connection with his fanbase. His fans, affectionately referred to as "Wallen's Warriors," remained a devoted and supportive group throughout the changes and controversies. Their loyalty was a testament to the genuine bond Wallen had formed with them through his music, his openness, and his willingness to acknowledge his mistakes.

Jerry Clarke

Social media played a significant role in Wallen's relationship with his fans, providing a platform for direct communication and interaction. Despite the occasional turbulent moments, his fanbase stood by him, recognizing that his journey was a human one, filled with highs and lows. Their unwavering support allowed Wallen to keep moving forward, knowing that he had a community that believed in his ability to grow and learn from his experiences.

In addition to his connection with fans, Wallen continued to work on his music, releasing new singles and exploring different aspects of his artistry. His willingness to experiment with his sound, blend genres, and explore new lyrical themes showed a depth and creativity that kept fans engaged and curious about what he would do next.

As Wallen's music evolved, so did his role within the country music community. He continued to collaborate with other artists, expanding his creative horizons and contributing to the vibrant tapestry of the genre. These collaborations allowed him to learn from his peers, share different perspectives, and create music that resonated with an even broader audience.

Wallen's commitment to growth and positive change was further evidenced through his involvement in philanthropic endeavors. He used his platform to raise awareness about important social issues, support charitable organizations, and make a positive impact on the world beyond music. His actions mirrored his desire to use his influence for the betterment of society, showcasing the maturation of an artist who understood the significance of his position.

In the grand narrative of Wallen's journey, the evolution of his image, his connection with fans, his musical exploration, and his dedication to making a positive difference all played crucial roles. The decision to shed the mullet, though seemingly a superficial change, carried deeper implications, representing a willingness to adapt, grow, and keep the focus on what truly matters—his music and the impact he could have on the world.

As we close the final chapter, we reflect on Wallen's remarkable story—a narrative of redemption, resilience, and an unwavering quest for personal and artistic growth. Beyond the melodies, Wallen seized his platform to sow the seeds of positive change, touching hearts and inspiring minds.

Morgan Wallen's odyssey serves as a living testament to the profound transformative influence that music wields, intertwining with his own evolution as a human being. His story is far from its conclusion, destined to carry forth with an enduring impact on the realm of country music and far beyond. Through the highs and lows, Wallen's journey resonates as a potent reminder of the remarkable power of both artistic expression and personal growth, a story that continues to unravel, imprinting an indelible mark upon the heart of our world.

Conclusion

As we bring "Morgan Wallen's Revolution: A Fresh Look" to a close, we reflect on the remarkable odyssey of an artist who has not only captured the hearts of millions with his music but has also undergone a profound transformation, emerging stronger, wiser, and more committed to making a positive impact on the world around him.

Through the pages of this biography, we have witnessed the early years of Morgan Wallen, growing up in the picturesque town of Sneedville, surrounded by the harmonious melodies of his musical family. We've learned about the pivotal role his father, a beloved preacher in their close-knit community, played in shaping his passion for

Morgan Wallen's Revolution: A Fresh Look

music and instilling in him a deep moral compass. These formative experiences not only laid the foundation for his musical journey but also set the stage for the remarkable person he would become.

As Wallen ventured beyond the hills of East Tennessee to pursue his dreams in Nashville, we were privy to the challenges and opportunities that awaited him in the heart of the country music universe. The early chapters of his career were marked by his undeniable talent, his dedication to honing his craft, and the unwavering support of his family. We saw how he navigated the competitive music scene, faced rejections, and used setbacks as motivation to become not just a good singer but a great artist.
However, Wallen's journey was not without its trials, and perhaps the most significant moment of reckoning was when a video surfaced in early 2021, showing him using a racial slur. This incident thrust him into a media firestorm, leading to a pivotal moment in his career and life. It was a moment of truth, a test of character, and a lesson in the power of accountability. Instead of shying away from the controversy, Wallen faced it head-on. He engaged with organizations and individuals working to promote racial understanding and equality. He sought education, he learned, he listened, and he took tangible steps toward positive change.

The artist's resilience during this challenging period was a testament to his character. He used the experience to grow, to learn about the historical context and significance of the word he used, and to actively contribute to the ongoing dialogue about diversity and inclusion. His commitment to using his platform for good, advocating for social causes, and promoting positivity showcased a profound sense of responsibility—one that was far beyond the realm of music.

As Wallen's personal growth unfolded, his music continued to serve as a beacon of connection, comfort, and inspiration for his fans. His ability to capture the essence of love, loss, and the complexities of life in his songs resonated deeply, transcending the boundaries of genre. His live performances remained powerful, further cementing his status as a gifted performer capable of captivating audiences with his raw emotion and unmatched stage presence.

One of the most intriguing elements of Wallen's journey was the evolution of his image, culminating in the dramatic decision to bid farewell to his iconic mullet. This symbolic change was not just about a hairstyle—it was about embracing transformation, a fresh start, and a recognition that growth requires adaptation. Wallen's willingness to evolve while staying true to his roots mirrored his personal evolution and his commitment to a journey of continuous improvement.

Throughout this biography, we've witnessed Wallen's interactions with his fans, the "Wallen's Warriors." Their unwavering support has been a driving force, a reminder that an artist's impact goes far beyond the music they create. Wallen's willingness to engage with his fans, to be open about his journey, and to acknowledge his mistakes has further solidified this bond. He's not just a musician to them; he's an inspiration, a figure who represents the power of perseverance and authenticity.

As Wallen's story continues to unfold, there is no doubt that he will continue to navigate the complexities of the music industry. The next chapters of his biography will reveal how he sustains his role as a beloved figure among fans, how he uses his platform to inspire positive change, and how he leaves an indelible mark on the world of country music and beyond.

The tale of Morgan Wallen's journey is a testament to the transformative power of both music and personal evolution. It's a story that showcases the strength of character, the resilience to overcome adversity, and the commitment to growth. It's a story that proves that an artist's impact goes far beyond the notes and lyrics—they have the power to shape lives, inspire change, and leave a legacy that extends beyond the boundaries of fame.

In closing, "Morgan Wallen's Revolution: A Fresh Look" is not just a biography; it's a celebration of the human spirit, a reminder that growth is a continuous process, and that even in the face of challenges, redemption is possible. Wallen's journey serves as an inspiration to all those who face obstacles, who grapple with mistakes, and who strive to become better versions of themselves. May his story continue to resonate, and may it inspire us all to embrace change, seek growth, and use our own platforms for positive transformation.

Made in the USA
Middletown, DE
15 March 2025